FOR
Paddy,Adam,Ewan,
Ashlie and Holly.
My parents,family and
My darling wife.

Foreword

This is for anyone who has a desire to leave society behind and live their lives with their complete freedom unaffected.For anyone who is not so sure how to make a dream like this happen and needs guidelines.
I had wanted for years to walk a way and move to the wild like I had seen in countless TV Shows and documentaries but never had a clue just how to go about it, so I just went and figured out the do's and really don't s once I arrived.
I left society behind and lived a tricky 4 years firstly in my car which I might add was a mistake then I grew some balls and went for it at full speed.
It wasn't easy but for 90% of the time it was certainly fun and always interesting.
I will share with you the different ways to completely disappear and avoid been spotted or captured if that's your objective.

In our increasingly volatile world its no wonder people are looking to break away from the fear and terrors that society forces on us.
With my experiences you can do it the way I never could.Yes it's likely you will make mistakes but if it was easy then it wouldn't be worth doing.

So if your a criminal trying to escape the clutch of law enforcement or a doomsday prepper looking for a little guidance to get you on your way this is for you.

****

DISCLAIMER.
This is a how to educational work.
The author does not take any responsibility for anyone's actions
whom have read this work and does not condone any criminal activity.

PLANNING

Planning is probably the most important step in this whole journey because without proper planning you are setting yourself up for failure or even death. If it's a case your running from the law then your planning will be limited and so this book is most likely going to be your getting away Bible!

Plan this out over a few months so as to make sure you have everything ready to go when the time is right.More than likely what ever your reason to want to break away from social Attention you will want to be able to and not be found. This takes effort.Avoiding suspicion of your imminent departure is key. If people don't know ,they can't inform on you and have your wonderful new life retracted before it's even begun.Your best friends and your loving family in this scenario can't be trusted and as much as you love them should be kept in the dark. So avoiding suspicion that your going to be going is first. You are going, so you have to play the mind games here. The people around you are Going to notice your absence once you suddenly up and leave so you need to start working a plan to keep them from going all Donnie brasco and calling in the feds and putting you on the missing persons list as this will cause you headaches and cause them heartache.So to begin with start by talking about taking a trip in a few months, you want to get away and find yourself or some such babble , your thinking Italy , Spain or joining a Buddhist temple in Asia.Its just loose talk at the moment but it puts a seed in the minds of the people who will worry most once you pack up and join this big green beautiful world we have in our back yard.

After a few weeks you will want to start talking about the reason you don't want to own a cell phone, you can't afford it, some research you read online about some rubbish, or you just feel you can't be bothered to give a fuck and all the while talking about your trip.During this time you will secretly be acquiring all the necessary kit you will need to bring with you to manage survivalism in sometimes harsh weather .(Don't worry it's not only to survive You will thrive) but we will look at kit later.

At this point you will need to create an identity.You will need to be someone new that your loved ones and depending on your legal situation an identity that your foe the police won't be able tie to you. A realistic sounding name is good and something your comfortable keeping because your going to need to own it and get used to it fairly fast.You will want a back story of your passed, don't go overboard with it you were never king of Some crazy country. Just keep it boring and basic but do make it believable.

EXAMPLE :
Name : Brian Jones .(FAKE NAME)
DOB : Fake it but keep the year real.
BORN: Opposite end of the country.

BIO : My name is Brian, Im from a small town nobody ever heard of (found online maps) , I went to a school in that small ass town (find the town online and find the name of the school) I worked in McDonald's for 3 years and felt trapped by the man so decided to go travel the world and find my way in life and bla bla bla.Ive just come out of a serious relationship but he/she cheated on me and completely destroyed me inside so on to new experiences ....
You get the point !!

Learn your back story and do not deviate from it, you will need it and if your writing down information then make sure it's hidden and nobody will see it then once your confident you have it in your mind burn it and leave no Trace.
The next step is going have you feeling like James Bond , you need identification to back up your sweet assed back story.This is not impossible but depending on your situation it is very important. You will need to get a passport in your new name.Its perfectly legal , once you change your name by deed poll and you can then really become the new person and leave behind the passed you want to desperately get away from.There are different ways of doing this depending on what country and state your in but I'll
be focusing on America, Britain and Ireland.

AMERICA:

There are generally three ways to change your name:

Usage – In some states using a name as your own has the effect of making it your name.

Order – A court order is recommended to change your name and is required by most states.

A marriage certificate serves as proof of name change.

You will need :

Your name as listed on birth certificate or immigration or citizenship documents.

The full name you are applying to change to (if you are changing your name).

* Date and place of birth

* Marital status and details

* Places of residence for last three months

* Address for Correspondence

Required documents:

* Certificate of Criminal Record

*Request Addressed to the Minister of Justice

* Application addressed to the Registrar

*Identity Card (original and photocopy

For the complete process check online and get it done in the early stages of planning.

BRITAIN:

Visit deedpoll.org.uk and you can do it all from there.

IRELAND:

You need visit
http://www.courts.ie/offices.nsf/0/B43B2E45023B633B802573D10045B030?O penDocument
For all your information.

So once you have gotten your new name and it's all official and remember nobody is aware of it then the trick is to go and get yourself a nice brand new passport to get out of your country or indeed to prove your not the person the feds are looking for if your stopped and asked for identification.
If a warrant is out on you it will be in your old name and also if a missing persons file is listed then it will also be in your old name.
Follow all the usual passport steps and attach your copy of your new name and keep an eye on the post so you get it and not your family members as it will be sent in your new name.

So with that bit of excitement done and securely packed away you will need another piece of identification, this one is a lot less hassle.
Online there are many websites available that make up plastic ID cards with your photo on they are cheap and usually good quality. You want to purchase one of these cards in a third name.Examples of the type of card you could get are : Student ID, library card, business ID.The reason for this is so if things get a bit tricky once you are away on your journey and you need to show identification but don't want to show your passport the 3rd ID is ideal and will throw people off the scent .Remember that through all your planning , especially if you are a fugitive to keep all your plans and details to yourself ,you can't trust anyone and if the price is right then they will rat you out!

We have looked at the process of making you disappear in name so far but now we must focus on making you disappear in body.
LOCATION LOCATION LOCATION.... Yes location is the next step to consider. I suggest you go onto an online map website and have a look around , ideally you want to be far from civilization to avoid been disturbed or even arrested. You will need shelter so a wooded area is great but you will need a location to be able to hunt animals, find drinking Water, vegetation to forage and even a way to fish for food if possible.

For Ireland I would suggest heading to the west of the country or even going over the water tothe UK .For the UK I would strongly suggest going far north into Scotland as they are more accepting of people living wild .
For the united States get to Alaska if you feel you can manage the weather but failing that head south over the boarder.

Ultimately you want to be more that 3 miles from any form of civilization so you can go about your life unaffected by society.

Planning your route there is an important part of this major life changing decision.There is no point in taking all the travel options that society provides because that is howYou can / will be tracked.
Leave your car at home or sell it because you will be caught on ANPR CCTV cameras equipped with software to take pictures of vehicles as they travel on roads and motorways. The numbers on the photos are then electronically cross-referred to databases used by the police .
You could use the money for your new life and the kit that be needed. You will need to stay off main roads and motorways to avoid anyone seeing you although it is inevitable that your going to be seen at some stage you should make it as little as possible,so hitchhiking is a pretty bad idea if your trying to avoid detection.So stick to minor roads and go through fields as much as you can. If your not much of a Walker then a push bike is ideal you can carry your gear easier and get to your final location Faster. I prefer to walk though as I get to see more of the land I'm travelling through and can Spot good locations to bed down and rest for the night and spot my food grazing on the land.
Try to keep an element of paranoia its a natural human instinct and will keep you from makingmistakes that could and should be avoided.

Don't forget taking a bus or train will leave you open to been recognized and your face caught On CCTV.
Use the legs God gave you and you stand a better chance of not been caught out.

On a side note: Irish and UK nationals can use the plastic identification to cross the irish sea on the ferry services, you don't need a passport (2016)

EQUIPMENT

In this section I'll discuss the kit and equipment I choose to bring with me and the reasons why so I'll leave a list first and then go through some of it.I choose Amazon to get most of mine.

* Hiking bag
* Sleeping bag
* Tent
* Tarpolin(s)
* Cooking mess set
* Flint striker / ferrocerium rod
* First aid kit
* Water containers
* Hammock
* Rope / para cord
* Travel compass
* Knives
* Axe (short handle)
* Sharpening stones
* Sewing kit
* Fishing kit

Backpack For your back pack you will need something large and lightweight with shoulder straps and if possible a good frame to keep it solid .Get a good quality water resistant material .The size I would recommend is 120 litres.
 Your tent is important until you manage to find a place that you will be able settle for the long term and able to build a cabin out of cut trees. Although you want something Lightweight you also need something that you can freely move about in and to store your gear.Choose a good water resistant material and a strong ground sheet. Avoid bright colours, try Go for camouflage greens.

Tarpolins are an important part of your equipment, it can be used on very rainy days to your tent and help to make sure that you get no leaks. It can be used to use as a to go on a guide wire over your hammock on warmer nights and also as protection a ground sheet. Once you start construction on your permanent shelter a tarpolin can used on the roof and walls to increase insulation. The bigger the better and again go a green camouflage to avoid been spotted.

Cooking mess sets are great for camping and living wild. I would suggest at least two mess tins to cook in, fork,knife,spoon and a canteen for water. They are made of aluminum usually and kits come in various sizes.

Flint striker/ ferrocerium rod is essential when living in the back and beyond. You may start out with matches or a lighter but the will soon get used up and you will be left sitting in the cold so a ferrocerium rod is your best bet here. There are many different types and sizes available but if you can pick up two fairly thick ones then you will be warm for a long time.

First aid kit. Living wild is a beautiful experience but from time to time you will end up with cuts and possibly worse so getting a few bandages, plasters and antiseptic spray is a great idea, a small cut in damp humid conditions untreated is a disaster and can lead to life threatening situations.

Water containers are great for keeping drinking water in your camp and to replenish your canteen once it's empty, also for cooking and cleaning with. You can get plastic fold away 1 gallon water containers very cheap and they will serve you well once you take care of them.

Hammock. In the summer months although sleeping in a tent or in your log cabin that you lovingly and carefully constructed is nice while in the woods or the field adjacent to it , sleeping in a hammock tied to a couple of trees is one of the most comfortable and amazing things you can experience while living wild. There are many variations of hammock out there so it's really personal preference which one if any you choose.

Rope / para cord. Most of the jobs you will come across in the wild will in some Way involve using rope to tie something together. Thicker rope is great for heavier chunky jobs but decent para cord has endless uses , for example holding your hammock to trees . Be careful when purchasing para cord as some retailers claim it's genuine military grade and it's not so do read the reviews from previous customers first.

Travel compass. You need to follow directions to find your camp and a compass is a Great way to help you figure your direction.

Knives. Here is your very best friend in the wild. You will use your knife in everything you do so finding a great quality knife is an absolute must. I say knives plural because one Is just not enough, you will have your one main knife but different jobs have different knives And so it's best to get an assortment to pack into your kit.

Axe . You will need to chop down trees to build with and chop up wood for your fire so an axe is another essential piece of your kit, alternatively you could get a nice handy travel saw but I would still recommend that you also have an axe.

Oil stones. So we covered the knives and axes previously but they are no use to you if they are blunt , you need to keep your tools maintained and using oil stones are the best way to sharpen your best Friend the knife.There are many different types of sharpening stones on the market but spending the little extra I find is usually worth it.

Sewing kit. The clothes you bring with you are eventually going to become torn andso having the kit available to you to mend them is very important. A cheap kit costs very little but saves you from a miserable time in the wild.

Fishing kit. There is not a need to bring a full fishing rod and reel as it will just be Extra weight you don't need however having a spool of fishing gut (line), some hooks and small weights is necessary to catch some tasty fish for dinner. You can make a reel from a waste bottle and wrap the line around it .

So with all that covered I want to suggest you purchase a "burner" cell phone. Yes I know some of you will be saying "what's this fool talking about ,that's how the feds willfind me" but wait.Taking a disposable phone with you and having the battery fully charged then put sticky tape over the battery connector ,replace the battery and it WILL NOT send out any signal or electrical current.So then why bring it? Well it's this simple,if you have a seriously bad accident and need help ,you can't get help with no way to communicate with the outside world. So it's in your bag nice and secure for emergencies.

Bringing a hunting tool is important in your new role as a hunter gatherer. Depending onyour location your options may be limited but in most states within the US you can just goget yourself a nice .22 rifle and that will be sufficient to kill small game like rabbits and squirrel.In the UK it is legal to buy a .22 gun without a license however the laws in Scotland are changing as of 1st January 2017 whereby you will be required to have a license for any and all firearms.In ireland you cannot own a firearm of any caliber without a licence , however there is an option, you can buy a bow and shoot arrows at your prey. There are different types of bow the most common being a longbow and compound bow, the latter being more suited to hunting.If taking hunting equipment remember to bring plenty of ammunition.

Your clothing is an important part of your equipment, its also an important part of you.Choosing the right type of clothing can really make or break a person in the wild.A nice warm fleece and thermal clothing is a must. Thick hiking socks are great too not Only for warmth but they are comfortable.
You will need some decent hiking boots, when your out hunting or finding new locations to make camp the boots will save your feet .Clothing I feel should be army camouflage green so you can be easily hidden and less likely to be noticed by animals your trying to catch and eat.Then some lighter clothes for the warmer days but I still suggest camouflage green!

FOOD TO START OUT WITH ,
 You should obviously bring a bit of food with you as you start out.
My suggestion is carry a few bags of oats, they are cheap and in the cold keep you warm,When tired it helps to boost your mood and with foraged berries they taste pretty good.

Chocolate is great too... When you have had a hard day walking or building and you feel Burnt out and you boil up some water and pine needles for your tea (pine needles are rich in Vitamin C) having a square of chocolate will definitely help boost your mood.

Coffee is a great luxury to have, waking up In your camp in the morning and brewing up a nice cup of coffee really helps to get you ready for the day that lies ahead.

Don't forget to bring your vegetables seeds to grow your own food and make it so you thrive and not just merely survive.
Don't be afraid of going hungry on your way you got the gift of dumpster diving at your hands as you go.Yes I said dumpster diving, you can find the best of food in the dumpsters in behind shops. It's just a case of getting brave and climbing in and finding your treasure.I've found some great stuff in dumpsters but use your head and obviously stay clear of meats and anything that's likely to make you sick.The other alternative for those of you that are more seasoned in survivalism is you are bound to come across "road kill", if it smells half decent then it's most likely fresh enough to skin and ready to throw onto a skewer and roast it on your lovely camp fire.You should be able to tell when it's cooked and ready to eat with a nice cup of pine needle tea

and trust me after the third time cooking up an animal and eating it ,knowing that you did it yourself and can rely on your new skills it gets a whole lot easier.You learn to really respect the land and animals you have available to you.

Don't bother bringing Canned food as it will dramatically increase the weight you have on your back and the more weight you have the quicker you will tire and the less ground you will cover.

PARANOIA

If your on the run from law enforcement then you will already know paranoia and that's a very good way to be.Its less likely you will be apprehend if your paranoid because you are more likely to be observant and so will avoid detection.The main thing is never get too complacent as this is where most people slip up and that's the end of the road for them.
So what's the best way to use your paranoia?Mobile phones are a no no because if you bring your regular mobile phone with you
The police or government can just use triangulation to get your location and believe me in this age they can pin point you mainly by using the GPS locators inside all android smart arse phones.Yes I know I said earlier to bring your burner but that's a new unregistered number that's never been used and with the tape on the battery it's essentially a dead device.

Money is another thing to consider.Avoid using any plastic, ATM machines have CCTV inside them and the machine registers that you have used it with the bank so if you use it and are a fugitive bye bye your caught, the same goes using a card in the shops, they all use CCTV to protect their premises and the recordings are digital so the footage of you being in the shop will be kept on the hard drive for quite some time.Cash is your friend, use only cash that you withdrew before you left and using a disguise a hat and sunglasses is usually enough to avoid been recognised but not a certainty

CCTV is EVERYWHERE, no matter where you go big brother is watching you so to avoid towns and cities it is essential to avoid being detected.
Using your map made of paper you can avoid walking into any built up area.
Cameras are outside shops ,banks , pubs and in shops ,bookies and florists so Naturally avoiding them is the best move.

Public Transport is another place CCTV is loaded up on so if you feel you need to take public transport then do so while in disguise.Remember though do NOT take the bus to take you out of your town as it's easier to be tracked once the authorities know where you started out from.So walk your ass a few miles out before taking public transport.

A side note on the CCTV is that police use face recognition equipment to identify criminals
so if your on camera and no disguise you will be easily traced.

If your deciding to take your car with you then again think twice. The car will be registered and so the police will be able track you down in minutes. The police use cameras that once Locked on to you your information is dropped on screen in police HQ and a unit will be despatched to your route and it's all game over.The cameras on bridges and speeding traps also use this technology so legs are generally better to avoid detection.

So now that your journey has begun and your into the big wide world you should start paying attention to your surroundings , you should start to see the different thing you can eat for example berries and nuts, you got nettles and some mushrooms so for the summer months you should gather and preserve all you can for the winter that will eventually arrive.I will post the names of books to consider buying to be able identify the correct items available in the wild that you can happily consume.

Check out any animals you see in fields, stop and watch their behaviour so you can get some sort of feel for how they move and how alert they are to danger so when your setting your dead fall trap you know what height is needed to kill the animal and where they like to feed.

You will also be on the look out for locations to sleep even if your not going to be staying there, to be able think in your mind that if I had to stay here what would I use and where.Its a great exercise to do while walking so it gets easier to find a good spot and helps to be faster at setting up your new home.

Look out for any houses and notice how far away the last ones were because the further you are from civilization the easier your life will be and less likely you will be caught.Farmhouses are likely to be well scattered out so doing a walk about or up a hill for a good vantage point to see your surroundings is a good idea

So now I bring you the other books that are very useful to help you when your out in The wild.

Food for free by Richard Mabey - pocket guide to what you can pick and eat in the countryside.(Mainly the UK and Ireland)

Mushrooms by Patrick Harding- pocket book to what are the edible mushrooms.

Tom Brown's field guide to wilderness survival- a guide showing survival techniques.

The rural ranger by Ron H Foster - shows how to build traps and snares.

Edible plants by Lee Allen Peterson - a guide to finding plants safe to eat (global)

Also it's worth checking You tube out for building cob houses and mud huts also Survival shelters .

In the end, you can only be successful at hiding away from the world if you truly make the effort and not give in to the natural instinct to make contact with loved ones.Many people have done this and been successful but more have failed. Going at it alone is a lonely adventure but if it's something that is deep inside you that wants to get out and try then remember the points written in this guide.

It worked for me, I'm writing this in my hut on my tablet right now, I'm somewhere in France and it's been four years , so this really is

THE PROVEN GUIDE TO LEAVE SOCIETY BEHIND!

Some pages now for you to make notes!

Notes :

Notes:

Notes:

Notes:

Notes: